Also by Jack Cady:

The Burning

(Iowa Press)

Dear Friends,

being

a letter to the I.R.S.

wherein the author

explicates

his non-compliance with

certain Federal tax regulations

and details

a number of Inalienable Rights

by

Jack Cady

a Copperhead chapbook

for the AMERICAN BICENTENNIAL *1776 - 1976*

Note: the author's contributor copies (ten per cent of the edition) have been donated to American Friends Service Committee at his request. --Ed.

Special thanks to Centrum Foundation, Port Townsend, Wa., where *Copperhead* is press-in-residence.

ISBN 0-914742-15-9

Copperhead
P. O. Box 271
Port Townsend, Washington 98368

Dear Friends,

March 27, 1975
Port Townsend, Washington
District Director of Internal Revenue
Seattle, Washington

Dear Friends:

Since we are about to become legal opponents I write to you something of myself and my beliefs in the hope that there may be understanding between us. I am resigned that there may never be agreement. Our rules conflict, but that does not mean that we cannot care for and respect the condition in which we find each other. Yours is a large agency of government. I want you to know that my quarrel is with the agency, not with anyone employed by the agency. What I must say in this letter about illegalities is directed to the agency and to our government. It is not directed to any single person or group of persons. That is one reason why I start with personal description and personal matters. I want you to know that I am not a statistic and that I do not consider any of you as nebulous, government enemies.

These were strange, windy days this winter. On the Washington Peninsula the rain held off through Christmas, the light on most days washed blue with touches of gold and red when I went downtown for morning coffee at a local cafe. When 1975 appeared it seemed that the wind picked up. The new year did not bring that much snow or rain, but the wail of the wind was like a continuing complaint. I reflected that it was not so much an ill wind, as a wind that complained of illness.

The wind kicks the high tide over the docks by the cafe. The water rolls in the channel, tumbling like a flow of gray, luminescent glass. By the door of the cafe is a newspaper rack. Before entering I always glance at the headlines and then try to think of something else. Sometimes I can succeed. It is a trick that a man picks up if he lives long enough.

The fact is that I really do not want to know what is happening in the rest of the world. What I really want is to live here in Port Townsend, work outside in all of our various weather, and watch the seasonal return of the water birds. Still, there is an exact appeal carried in those newspapers. They name people and events and places. The people are important. I think that most of them are not very different from myself. I enter the cafe knowing that if there is a loose paper about I'll surely read it.

Slurping coffee. Morning smoke. Turning pages, and feeling the presence around me of those of my neighbors who also start the day in this manner. Sometimes there is a tourist group. It is quiet and seems almost like a religious gathering although we drink coffee instead of breaking bread. I read the paper, reflect that for forty-three years I have loved my country, and also reflect that for forty-three years my country has been training me to go to prison. That is a difficult thing to accept and it is lonely. I turn the pages and realize how much of what I read is not news.

It is not news that there are insecure men in high places. It is not news that the business of armies is to kill. It is not news that large corporations regularly engage in criminal activities.

What is news is that conversations between military, government and industry are becoming more intelligible. As this happens decisions that affect us here in Port Townsend and which also affect citizens all over the world are made with no regard to anyone as human being or citizen. Our President speaks of future war while our young sons are getting older. In the cafe cynical remarks are sometimes made saying that once more the nation will be called on to make the world safe for Standard Oil. I hear those remarks and wonder if the speaker realizes that a new dictatorship is forming.

After reading as much as I can bear, I finish my coffee and leave. The truck I drive is old. It smells of loam and tree cuttings, of fertilizer and newly cut grass. The thing chugs up hills because the compression of the old engine is shot. It is a truck with good steering, good brakes, and little else. Even so, it is in better condition than our government.

My day's work may be grades or trees or plant beds. I'll be working with leaves and flowers, with soil and irrigation. I think that since I quit being a teacher this is another good and honest way to make a living. I drive down the road, past the new billboard that reminds our local kids that when eligible they must register for the draft, and first I am angry and then I am sad. The people of this town have no international enemies. These people did not appoint a government to make enemies for them. My neighbors are peaceable people and murder or violence around here is quite remarkable. We get along, and for the most part I think we like each other. Hatred is not in our streets, and hatred for people in like towns across the world is not in our hearts. That is one of the good reasons why I do not want to leave this place for the scurryings of a government that continually insists on my loyalty while negotiating destruction.

It seemed necessary to tell you this before our first

confrontation which will be the examination of my 1973 tax return. I expect the examination is prompted by my refusal last year to pay half of my income tax. I will refuse to pay half of the tax again this year, although because of withholding your agency already has most of the money. I refuse to pay half of the tax on various grounds, some of which are moral, some of which are legal. The refusal is prompted by the expenditure by our government of over fifty per cent of tax monies on the maintenance and purchase and use of armies and weapons. Through its agency, Internal Revenue Service, the United States government seeks my complicity in the violation of twenty centuries of moral teaching. The government is in further violation of various international treaties and agreements, and is, in fact, engaged in crimes against peace and crimes against humanity.

These are serious charges and I make them not with indignation but with a great deal of personal pain. This is my beloved country. I have studied its history, its songs; and I have taught its beliefs and ideals. I think I have understood the real determination of freedom and respect that hundreds of thousands of its people have worked so hard to gain for others as well as for themselves. I know something about its religions, its painting and philosophy, its architecture and its politics. It is terrible to have to make those charges, because I know what its people have dreamed and believe I know that the dreams of equality and truth are still valid and alive. This affair of the tax is a trap. Either I believe in the United States of America as bastion of the free spirit, or I quit believing and simply pay my taxes. I am grieved to say that these are the charges, and I am even more grieved to say that the charges are so simply proved as to be prima facia:

The first charge is moral. The nation claims to be a Christian nation. Its code is, "One nation under God," and it proclaims that "In God we trust." I have observed that this is not true.

The Christian and Hebraic injunction, "Thou shalt not kill," is specific. It does not carry exemptions. The U. S. record in Korea (when I was a conscientious objector) and the later record of Viet Nam demonstrates that the United States will kill at convenience. It will kill combatants and non-combatants alike. It will do so under the banner of maintaining a free world or to make people free, usually from the clutches of communism. In doing so, and without consulting the peoples involved, it will use bombs, gasses, explosives and napalm to destroy children. This is the record, and the record continues to be endorsed by the U. S. weaponry in Viet Nam and Cambodia. No morality can attach to such action no matter what plea is given that U. S. political theory is more sacrosanct than other political theories. I do not see that the much inflated communist bear is less immoral than demonstrated U. S. action in killing children. To answer that our nation must be immoral because other nations are immoral is to align us exactly on the same level of violence and degradation that the U. S. pretends to deplore.

In addition, it is increasingly clear that economics and not the threat of communism is the force that keeps our military so well supplied. The irony of the imprint, "In God we trust," is on our coins; but now, even our coins are watered with base metal between slivers of silver. It has only marginally to do with my objection, but I will point out that our current economic ills derive from incredible overspending which certainly aids and abets communist governments. If there is competition with those governments then it is clear the U. S. will eventually lose. It will not lose through military engagements but through moral and economic bankruptcy. When a free people fears to depend on their moral strength and turn instead to weapons stockpiling then it is certain that expensive and very inadequate insurance is being purchased.

In writing that is usually reprinted as "An Essay on Slavery", Thomas Jefferson pointed out that the enslavement of human beings degraded not only those enslaved, but degraded the masters. His moral observation was exact. He pointed out that when one person is placed about another in such a relationship the dehumanization and brutalization was as strong for the master as for the slave. He wrote, "I tremble for my country when I reflect that God is just." Approximately two hundred years later moral issues of the same import are before us. The first one is simply stated. The U. S. is still dealing in a kind of slavery by its dealings and support involving enslaving governments.

The second issue is internal. The U. S. is supporting destruction of national wealth to maintain not only an artificial way of life, but to maintain a false economy through useless and destructive weaponry and war. As I comprehend it, the issue is exactly this: The U. S., given its then unique economic and philosophic attitudes, could not fail in its beginnings to become a great nation. It could not fail because its natural resources literally did seem inexhaustable.

We know better now. The resources are exhaustable and many of them are nearly exhausted. Last year, doing research, I came to a realization of just how desperate the circumstances already are. The nation is clearly running out of petroleum, crop land and water. More crop land and water will be destroyed because of the extraction and processing of coal. I can demonstrate all this, although it is not necessary at the time. I will say that one great issue of the next ten years is the issue of water. Meanwhile, in order to support an artificial economy the nation continues to plow millions of tons of coal, steel, precious metals and hundreds of thousands of acre feet of water into machines of destruction. The U.S. spends its real wealth in resources demonstrating to the world that it is too weak to depend on its moral strength.

We paid for slavery with the self destruction that was the Civil War. I fear that we will pay as greatly for our current self destruction. Already there is trouble among us. Once, Americans were concerned with living. Now many of our people seem only concerned with not dying.

The rest of the points of my objection are legal. They are:

In requiring that I pay taxes for the support of war, planning for war, offensive weapons and the maintenance of a standing armed force sufficient to engage combat on a worldwide scale, the U. S. government through its agent I.R.S. is in violation of the First Amendment to the Constitution which guarantees my religious freedom. I am a member of the Port Townsend meeting for worship of the Society of Friends, Quaker. The Quaker belief and effective detachment from war dates from the beginnings of the society in the middle 1660s. The precedent of refusal to pay war taxes in America dates from 1755 when John Woolman, John Churchman and Anthony Benezet refused to pay for the French and Indian wars. Nonviolence and refusal to pay or endorse either side in a combat dates in U. S. history from the revolution when Quakers who refused to kill were stoned or beaten under the brand of Tory. I claim my devout belief in God and the injunction that we may not kill as sufficient reason to refuse this tax. I would expect that opposition to this view would also have to overcome three hundred years of Quaker nonviolence, and two hundred years of U. S. acceptance of Quaker attitudes that insist on nonviolence.

The second point of objection is that the U. S. is in violation both historically and presently of the Geneva

Accords. The accords are specific and so are the violations. They involve not only the control and killing of civilians, but the importation of weapons into a country and the manipulation of populations including the fifty per cent of population that are now refugees in Cambodia.

The third point is that in asking taxes, the U.S.A. through its agent I.R.S. seeks my complicity in crimes against peace and crimes against humanity as defined by the Nuremberg Principles. These principles hold that a citizen of a nation is guilty of crimes committed by his nation if he acquiesces to those crimes when, in fact, a moral choice is open to him. A moral choice is open to me, and to endorse U. S. actions in perpetrating crimes against humanity is to announce in terms of the Nuremberg Principles that I am co-author of those crimes. I would detail such crimes, but they are numerous and can be detailed later as necessary. They have to do with destruction of non-combatants, destruction of villages, introduction of illegal weapons; in fact, they read like the newspapers.

The fourth point is that the U. S. is in violation of the Hague Conventions on several points including the use of poison gasses. (Also a violation of the Nuremberg Principles.) The current argument of "first use" is no more than political flummery. A nation that historically proved it will use atomic weapons may assume no legal validity by saying that it will not use gas until some other nation uses gas. I am sorry to say that the argument very much resembles the statement by a homicidal maniac that he will not kill again; this in spite of the fact that his psychological condition seems to have deteriorated.

In proof of the above point, the Pentagon request for fiscal year '75 is for $107 million for research and development of biological warfare. The military is currently defying a Congressional ban on the production of a specific nerve gas known as GB, and another known as

VX. Either cause instantaneous death on contact with the skin. I think you can understand why many people would not want their taxes to be paying for this sort of thing.

The fifth point is that the U.S.A. is in violation of the United Nations Charter, Article 1, sections 2, 3 and 4.

The sixth point is that the U. S. in stockpiling weapons, planning for war, and maintaining a large military force is in violation of our basic law and international law deriving in this nation from English law. It is a long accepted principle taught in law schools all over the country, and supported by the courts when it becomes an issue. The law derives originally from the writing of Thomas Hobbs. It states that the duty of the citizen to the state ceases when the state fails to protect, and actually threatens the life of the citizen. At this point, the citizen has not only the right but the obligation to resist.

In requiring that I pay taxts to support a war industry and armed forces capable of contending on a worldwide scale, the U. S. Government is threatening both my moral and physical existance. I am not being protected because the U. S. builds atomic weapons, B-1 bombers, atomic submarines, poison gas, lasers, ricketry, napalm and all of the other expensive paraphernalia of war. These do not protect me. They invoke the suspicion and fear of other nations and they provoke among other nations the building and stockpiling of similar weapons. Despite the assurance of manufacturers that these weapons are to make us strong and free, it is easy to sec that they make us weak and vulnerable. They endanger the life of every U. S. citizen. I do not wish to be redundant, but weapons get used. The U. S., by record, has used atomics, poison gas, napalm, indiscriminate bombing against civilian tarets and fielded armies that were of women and children. The nation has proved that it will use its weapons. I see no reason why any other nation on earth should trust a U. S. promise of non-use. This threatens my life. My nation no longer qualifies as protector. I owe no allegience to tax rules designed ultimately to destroy me and those whom I love. In fact, under our law, I have the obligation to refuse.

My final, legal objection is that the U. S. now gives every indication that it is, in fact, not a nation of laws but a nation of men and corporations. This, despite the resignation from office of Richard Nixon and Spiro Agnew. I charge that the freedom of the citizen is largely illusory, and that the payment of taxes, the keeping of tax records the invasion of privacy by I.R.S. and other agencies of government, the making of rules by agencies (rules that have the force and effect of law but which are not to be challenged in courts), the maintenance of records or files on the political, religious, economic and moral statements and actions of the individual, the power to levy fines and license by agency rule, and the presumption by government that the citizen is guilty of any agency charge and must therefore bear the burden of proof of his innocence; all of these show that the citizen of the U. S. is no longer free.

I have two main intentions in this tax refusal. The first is quite clear. I do not intend to pay for the destruction of other human beings, nor endorse by word or deed the crimes of the United States. The second intent is a little more nebulous but it is just as strong. It is strong because I love my country.

In this refusal I intend that the United States will display by its actions whether a citizen, raised to believe in U. S. principles of freedom, equality, protection under the laws; raised in fact, under statements like, "With a proper regard for the opinions of mankind," can indeed trust and believe in the way he has been raised. Either the Constitution is sound or it is not. The U. S. will either honor its national and international committments or it will not. The courts will either face the issues or the courts will duck them.

Having loved this country for forty-three years it is now time for the country to either prove worthy of my regard and dedication, or it is time for it to show that what I've been taught (and what I have taught hundreds of others in American literature and American studies classes) is indeed a fraud. If the rules of I.R.S. are bigger than the Constitution, the U. N. Charter, the Nuremberg Principles and the Christian teaching of two thousand years then I believe it is time that the U. S. acknowledge this. At least the citizen would not be damaged, as I may have been, by illusions of truth, equality and freedom. I hope, in fact, that this nation may prove worthy of its beginnings as it approaches its two hundredth year. I hope that men like Jefferson, Woolman, Franklin and Penn were not wrong, and that their support of laws and ethical principles was not misplaced. I hope that it proves true that these principles are greater than the opportunistic violences wrought under the excuse of various crisis.

Please schedule my appointment at any convenient time, since I am no longer on jury duty. While I have more than adequate records I will appear without those records. As you probably know, the maintenance of records and the requirement that I show the records are in clear violation of the Fifth Amendment to the Constitution. Also I believe you may be in violation of your own regulations although I am unsure of this particular point. The letter I received also asked for information on my '72 return. As I understand it, your regulations allow you to see only one return. Then, if errors become evident, you may request others; although you may not go beyond the Statute of Limitations unless fraud is indicated. Will you please clarify this by letter? I assure you that you will not be able, no matter how many obscure rules, to find indication of fraud. However, I have been told by one I.R.S. employee that the rules are interpretable in such a way that he could find something wrong with my tax return, no matter when filed or by whom. This, and my past experience in calling I.R.S. and getting contradictory verbal opinions from two or even three I.R.S. employees makes me believe that both the agency and myself will be in a much stronger position if I come with a tape recorder and accompanied by a witness.

Thank you for your attention to this long letter. I hope that we can treat humanely with each other, dealing in terms of respect and kindness and that a great deal of understanding and learning may pass between us. Perhaps even our country will derive some small benefit, since finally, it is the condition and stance of this nation that I take to be in question.

Jack Cady

1000 COPIES designed & printed at Copperhead using Linotype Fairfield text with Baskerville display. The papers are Beckett.

12 COPIES have been handbound in cloth and hand-marbled paper over boards by The Watermark.

Pamphleteers of 1776 were often under a great sense of urgency because their material was immediate and their cause an appeal to their fellows as well as an appeal to heaven. They occasionally made printer's errors. We are glad to report that some things remain constant in human experience.

ERRATA

less immoral --	less moral
Hobbs --	Hobbes
ricketry --	rocketry
fielded armies that were -- of women and children	fielded armies against women and children